Services *for the* urban poor

Services *for the* urban poor

5.

From Action Plans to Implementation

Andrew Cotton & Kevin Tayler

Water, Engineering and Development Centre
Loughborough University
2000

Water, Engineering and Development Centre,
Loughborough University,
Leicestershire, LE11 3TU, UK

ISBN 13 Paperback: 978 0 90605 582 3
ISBN Ebook: 9781788533478
Book DOI: http://dx.doi.org/10.3362/9781788533478

A catalogue record for this book is available from the British Library.

A reference copy of this publication is also available online at:
http://www.lboro.ac.uk/wedc/publications/sftup.htm

Cotton, A.P. and Tayler, W.K. (2000)
Services for the Urban Poor:
Section 5. From Action Plans to Implementation
WEDC, Loughborough University, UK.

WEDC (The Water, Engineering and Development Centre) at Loughborough University
in the UK is one of the world's leading institutions concerned with education, training,
research and consultancy for the planning, provision and management of physical
infrastructure for development in low- and middleincome countries.

This edition is reprinted and distributed by Practical Action Publishing.
Since 1974, Practical Action Publishing has published and disseminated books and
information in support of international development work throughout the world. Practical
Action Publishing trades only in support of its parent charity objectives and any profits are
covenanted back to Practical Action (Charity Reg. No. 247257, Group VAT Registration No.
880 9924 76).

This document is an output from project R7292 funded by the UK Department for
International Development (DFID) for the benefit of low-income countries.
The views expressed are not necessarily those of DFID.

Acknowledgements

The financial support of the Department for International Development of the British Government is gratefully acknowledged. The authors would particularly like to thank their many urban engineering colleagues and friends throughout India, Pakistan and Sri Lanka with whom they have worked for the last fifteen years. Their experience has been central to the preparation of this work. Mr P Srinivasa Rao from Hyderabad, India provided a critical review of earlier drafts and additional material for Sections 4 and 6. Colleagues at WEDC and GHK Research and Training provided information and comments throughout the development of the work. We also acknowledge the inclusion of some material from earlier work jointly authored with Dr Richard Franceys. Finally, we wish to acknowledge Sue Cotton for her editorial contributions and the patience and skill of Rod Shaw and Glenda McMahon of the WEDC Publications Office in the design and production of the manual.

Contents

Section 5

From Action Plans to Implementation

Who should read this

- Local Infrastructure Programme Managers and Executive Engineers who are responsible for developing and implementing Action Plans for improved services for the poor in towns and cities.
- Infrastructure Programme Managers from the donor agencies and technical support partners including NGOs and local/international consultants. The overall principles outlined in this section will also be of interest to Project Directors and other Programme Sector Managers (for example: Community Development; Health) who need to be familiar with the ideas underlying the programme for improving services.

Objectives of this section

To provide guidance on how to take the Local Action Plans forward to the stage of implementing service improvement at the field level. This focuses on the development and use of administrative procedures for technical and financial approval and the different options for procurement and contracting in order to deal with the potentially very large number of small improvement works which will arise.

Please note that some of this material on government procedures is included for the benefit of those who are providing technical support but are not familiar with the principles of government procurement procedures; government engineers will be well versed in this.

What this section tells you

The **source of finance** for the service improvements is a key factor in determining what approval procedures are required in order to implement proposals on the ground.

For an upgrading programme implemented through government, it is important **not to invent new procedures** which are significantly different from those which are commonly used; otherwise the strategic approaches to planning will be lost once the programme ends.

Local Action Plans for many different communities mean that there are potentially thousands of different small works to implement. **Streamlining approval and financial procedures** is therefore essential.

This can be assisted by developing **standard engineering details** with standardised unit costs for a wide range of technical options.

Cost estimating spreadsheets can be developed from the standard engineering details; these can be used for rapid assessments of costs of different options during local action planning.

Confusion sometimes arises because government engineers **estimate costs** according to their local Schedule of Rates; this may be different from current market rates. Both can be dealt with if cost estimating spreadsheets are developed.

Construction work can either be managed conventionally by government engineers using contractors, or community groups can become directly involved in construction and management of minor works in their neighbourhood.

Quality control can be a major problem and effective, independent monitoring is essential. Involving user and community groups can strengthen this process.

Administrative procedures

The Local Action Plan contains a list of improvement works which have been developed in a participatory way for each of the sectors; these have been agreed with the key agencies and local political representatives during the consensus building process described in Section 3c. The technical options and financing arrangements have also been agreed as part of the local action planning process.

The next step is to turn each of the recommended actions into a 'work package' which ultimately becomes a contract for implementing the service improvements. We need formal procedures to establish very clearly who is going to do what and how they are going to do it. A useful starting point is to consider how this takes place within the government system. The procedures described in Table 5.1 are the standard everyday practice of technical staff of most Public Works Departments and its principles are used by most government implementing agencies.

Table 5.1. Public Works Departments (PWD) procedures

Narrative	Commentary
1. A scheme needs to be formulated. This need not necessarily be done by the Department; their approval and procurement procedure starts once the requirements of the scheme have been put before it, regardless of their origin.	■ In our case, local action planning is the means by which the schemes are formulated.
2. Preliminary cost estimates are prepared.	
3. These estimates are approved by the Department; this is termed *administrative approval*.	■ In general, the basis here is 'rule of thumb' and past data.
4. The necessary surveys, plans and designs are drawn up by the Department's engineers.	
5. Detailed cost estimates are prepared on the basis of these plans.	■ The basis of these cost estimates is the government approved Schedule of Rates (SoR) and approved details. PWD is the main source of reference.
6. These estimates are approved by the appropriate officials in the Department; this usually involves the Chief Engineer; this is termed *technical sanction*.	
7. The work is *awarded;* there are a number of options available for implementing construction of the infrastructure.	■ See later section: the preference in government is always for competitive bidding.
8. Completion of construction and *finalisation of work*.	■ Marked by the last entry of the measurement book, as reflected in the completion certificate.
9. Completion and end of the *defect liability* period.	

Sources of finance

The source of finance is a very important factor in relation to the administrative procedures and rules which need to be adopted for approving expenditure on service improvement works identified in the Local Action Plans. Table 5.2 identifies the requirements.

Table 5.2. Whose money is it?	
Source of finance	**Rules and procedures**
Government	Government money is used to finance the works in the Local Action Plan; their procedures need to be followed in approving expenditure.
External Donor Agency	External donor agencies provide the finance for the works with the money being channelled through the government; again, government procedures need to be followed and it is also likely that the donor will require additional procedural stages.
Users and community groups	Government money is not involved; the finance is raised internally by service users and community groups. They are at liberty to define and use whatever mechanisms they feel confident with. Relatively little reliance is placed on the written word and trust between the partners is the key.
Split financing	Split funding using the 'matching grant' approach with contributions from government and community groups. The government agency will need to ensure that its procedures are followed, and the community will need to be confident that it knows what is happening to its own money.

There are two procedural possibilities.

1. Develop a new set of streamlined procedures which are tailor-made for the upgrading programme and cut out the apparent bureaucracy of government. The justification for this is that the local action planning process is participatory and the plan has gone through a consensus building phase involving a wide group of stakeholders; also, the donor finance is external to the government.
2. Work within the existing procedures outlined in Table 5.1; use the Local Action Plan as the means of 'formulating' a scheme and then follow the Departmental procedures in obtaining the necessary approvals.

The first option is attractive at first sight, but there are serious drawbacks. One of the underlying objectives of an upgrading programme which develops participatory and demand responsive planning is to try to bring such approaches into the mainstream of government activity in the urban sector. If new procedures are created for implementing the plans, then there is little chance that the improved approaches to planning will be widely adopted once the project has finished. Government staff will revert to using the standard procedures outlined in Table 5.1 and there will be no lasting impact in terms of process development.

Therefore, we strongly recommend that the implementation procedures for the Local Action Plans follow the established procedures of Table 5.1. In this way, government officials can see that the local action planning approach is compatible with their existing procedures and the way that they work in an administrative sense. This is important because government departments function almost entirely according to established rules and procedures; this is the way they will continue to work when outsiders have gone. These are understood by all concerned and there is nothing to be gained (and much to be lost) by attempting to by-pass them. Note that these procedures are not entirely static; it is possible to get minor amendments made to existing procedures. If new staff are drafted in to deal with the increased workload, it is essential to specify exactly who has the authority to approve what. The procedure may remain the same as recommended above, but it will be necessary to clarify the delegated authority of staff seconded to the programme.

We can now look at how to apply the general Departmental procedures outlined in Table 5.1 to the Local Action Plans.

Streamlining approval procedures

Each Local Action Plan may contain a considerable number of individual service improvements; multiply this for all of the different communities to be upgraded city wide and there are potentially thousands of different small works to implement. The following potential problems have all been observed in actual implementation of upgrading schemes:

- although we have a set of workable procedures to follow, it can be very time consuming to move through the various stages of approval, with all the attendant dangers of losing the confidence of the users and community groups;

- individual engineers tends to develop his/her own particular technical details, which means that no two pieces of work are exactly the same;
- each detail and its cost has to be checked and certified; this is time consuming;
- quality control becomes a problem.

Whilst a few municipalities have attempted to address these problems by standardising some of the design and cost estimation, the practice is not widespread for minor works.

One way of tackling the lack of standardisation in the design, estimation of quantities and costing is to develop a number of *standard engineering details* (SEDs) in the early stages of the upgrading programme. With this 'library' of SEDs it is possible to develop a streamlined 'once-only' approval procedure.

- The design and cost of each detail is agreed and approved at the outset by the municipality (assumed to be the government implementing agency) and the external donor agency (if it is providing finance and/or technical assistance).
- This means that subsequent approvals for work packages arising out of Local Action Plans can be made much simpler because the proposed works are based on these 'pre-approved' standard details and costs.

Table 5.3. illustrates how this can be adapted.

Table 5.3. Procedure for developing work packages from Local Action Plans			
What to do (procedural steps)	**How to do it**	**Who does it**	**Guidance**
Formulate a plan of work	This can be a simple statement of intention to proceed with development of Local Action Plans in specified localities.	Programme Manager after the identification of target neighbourhoods/groups is complete.	
Obtain administrative approval	This may only need to state the funds to be made available through government channels, possibly on a per capita or per area basis.	Engineer or Programme Manager with appropriate delegated authority in implementing department or committee at the consensus building stage.	

Table 5.3. (continued)

What to do (procedural steps)	How to do it	Who does it	Guidance
Prepare cost estimate	These are as specified in the Local Action Plans using SEDs and associated unit cost estimates. Make separate estimates using the Schedule of Rates and the local market rates.	Engineer; **detailed market rate cost estimates are agreed jointly with the service users**. This is an important amendment to the conventional approach; see following section on standardisation of cost estimation.	Tool 16, section on Cost information for user groups and communities
Obtain technical sanction	Present the Local Action Plan with its detailed cost estimates as a single package for approval.	Engineer or committee with appropriate delegated authority in implementing Department. Plan to be signed off by representatives of the beneficiaries.	Tool 16, section on Cost information for approvals and sanctions
Obtain donor sanction if applicable	The donor may wish to sanction specific expenditure as well as being involved at the consensus building stage which gives administrative approval to the Local Action Plans. **Market rate estimates need to be used here**.	Programme manager in donor agency with appropriate delegated authority.	Tool 16, section on Cost information for approvals and sanctions
Procurement and contracting	Decide on the procurement method. Note that for larger networked infrastructure work, individual contracts will be developed.	See Procurement and contracting section	Table 5.6

We now have a set of 'work packages' for the construction of engineering works relating to each of the service improvements for which expenditure has been approved where funds are being channelled through the municipality.

Standardisation of design

Local action planning provides the opportunity for service users to say what they want. Tool 6 describes possible technical options which will cover most circumstances and it is possible to use this to develop a range of standard items of infrastructure from which users can choose. These are known as standard engineering details, and in essence comprise:

- a description and drawing; and
- a unit cost estimate.

These standard details are of great help:

- they provide a straightforward way for service users to see what is available if they are presented simply and clearly;
- the standardised costs are readily available and service users can see how the costs of different options and levels of service can be traded off within an overall expenditure limit;
- overall quality control is improved through standardisation of the design, specification and costing of the different items of infrastructure;
- the design of the local improvements is no longer totally dependent upon the ability of the individual engineer assigned to the area; and
- many of the service improvements will be similar between different up-grading areas in the programme; standardised items helps to optimise the use of engineers time.

Note that this by no means implies that a common blue print solution is to be adopted across all areas. The local action planning approach determines user priorities and demand, giving a choice of actual items from the menu of options with an attached 'shopping list' of costs.

Please refer to Tool 15 which describes how to develop standard engineering details for use in an upgrading programme.

Standardisation of cost estimation

The granting of technical sanction for work to be carried out requires detailed cost estimates to be approved. The main effort goes into measuring up the work which needs to be done and estimating the costs involved according to the government approved Schedule of Rates. This gives unit cost details for most conceivable materials and civil engineering construction activities; the engineer then builds up an estimate for the cost of, say, cement concrete paving of a particular access way. If a donor agency is involved they will want to know how much is to be spent in order to ensure that particular project conditions are being met and for its own monitoring purposes. Whilst the proposals to be funded by user groups do not have to go through the above procedures, it is obvious that the users will want an accurate estimate of the cost. This is described in more detail in Table 5.4.

Table 5.4. Costs: Who needs to know what?		
Group	**Role in this context**	**What they need to know**
Users	Financing some of the proposals	■ how much the work will cost when completed ■ how the costs break down into skilled/unskilled labour and materials so that they can minimise the financial cost of construction by providing their own labour or hiring particular skills
Municipality	Implementing works and managing donor funding	■ the exact value of the work as estimated according to the Schedule of Rates in force at the time
Donor	Financing some of the proposals	■ how much the work will cost when completed ■ how close is the completion cost to the estimated budget cost

Therefore we have three groups all of whom need to know the cost of the works. The problem is that the Schedule of Rates rarely reflects the actual market price of getting things done; this is explained further in Table 5.5. Unfortunately this means that the cost estimation carried out by the municipality engineers is not actually of use to either the service users or the donors.

Table 5.5. The problem with PWD cost estimation: the Schedule of Rates	
Narrative	**Commentary**
1. Government engineers prepare detailed cost estimates for technical sanction	
2. These estimates have to be based on the latest edition of a Schedule of Rates (SoR) provided by the Public Works Department	■ this provides a standard basis for tendering
3. The SoR is updated periodically; the problem is that in practice many years may elapse between updates	■ high construction cost inflation means that the estimates rapidly become unrealistic
4. The cost estimates which are given technical sanction do not reflect the actual cost of procuring the works unless the SoR is up to date	■ if the actual cost of a contract increases beyond a certain limit then the approval process has to be repeated
5. The market rate for doing the work is therefore nearly always greater than the engineers' cost estimate	■ in one extreme case, the SoR was over 15 years old, with tender prices coming in at many times the estimated value
6. Prices tendered for work have to reflect the market rate	■ these estimates serve no purpose in terms of managing the work for the contractor

The preparation of cost estimates is an area where there is considerable scope to develop simplified procedures which can be used to assist in the development of the Local Plans as well to speed up PWD approval mechanisms. We need to have a system which reflects the information needs of the three groups as described in Table 5.4. The whole process of local action planning and implementation of works depends on sorting out a mechanism for cost estimation which gives all parties the information which they require.

Please refer to Tool 16 which describes how to develop simple spreadsheets for cost estimation using the idea of standard engineering details.

Deciding on market rates

A genuine problem arises in how to determine what costs to use to carry out market rate calculations; this becomes particularly important if work is going to be awarded other than by competitive tender. There are a number of possibilities.

- Update the Schedule of Rates at least annually so that there is no significant discrepancy between the SoR and the market. This does not appear to be realistic at present.

- Allow a percentage premium on the SoR for different items of work. This has been successfully adopted in some places, where an informal committee of Superintending Engineers for a particular circle/district meet every six months to test the market and agree specific premiums. These can be used in cost estimation and in the award of work through entrustment by negotiation or departmental works (i.e. other than by competitive tender). There is often reluctance to do this; in particular, external donors can be quite averse to anything which removes the element of competitive tendering as a means of market testing. This is all very well in a 'perfect market'; external people rarely understand the nature of the local market which may be far from perfect. Tender rates can be affected by the practice of 'pooling' by contractors.

Procurement and contracting

The procedures described in the previous sections turn the proposals from the Local Action Plans into specific work packages for infrastructure construction activities. The next stage is to award the work; there are a number of options for implementing the construction of infrastructure:

- the construction work is managed by the municipality, using one of a number of different procedures available, the most common of which is to award the work to an established contractor through a process of competitive tender;

- community groups are directly involved in construction work and/or in the management of the work in their neighbourhood.

A separately published tool is available which provides guidelines on the involvement of community groups in the infrastructure procurement process. Table 5.6 guides you to the relevant sections of *Community Initiatives in Urban Infrastructure* (A P Cotton, M Sohail and W K Tayler, 1997).

The main text also looks at the relative performance of community partnered works with those procured by conventional contract. This booklet is also available in Urdu and Sinhala.

Table 5.6. Guide to the relevant sections of *Community Initiatives in Urban Infrastructure*	
Guidance Point	**Section**
Community partnering in neighbourhood infrastructure	Section 2, p4-8
Urban Government procedures for awarding work to construct infrastructure	Box 2, p46
Roles and responsibilities of different partners: how community groups become involved in procurement	Section 4, p11-13
Working with government: users and community groups as advisers in conventional contracting	Box 10, p57
Working with government on a programme with split financing of service improvements: the community as partial promoter	Box 9, p54
Working without government with improvements financed by users: community as promoter	Box 7, p52
Guidelines for community partnered procurement: includes: ■ identifying the partners ■ roles for community groups ■ scope for partnering in procurement ■ identifying capacity for different roles ■ organisational status of community groups ■ identifying appropriate procedures ■ identifying procedures in urban government ■ cost estimation and access to finance ■ preparing to enter into agreements ■ selecting a contract type ■ negotiating a contract ■ documentation ■ sample form of agreement ■ managing community partnered micro contracts	Section 5, p25-41

Quality control, monitoring and construction cost

Quality control of construction work can be a serious problem; in some places, work carried out by government and its contractors has a poor reputation for quality. On the other hand, there is strong evidence that where community groups have been involved, the quality of work can be very good (see *Community Initiatives in Urban Infrastructure*). However, there are genuine concerns about lack of competition in situations where work has been awarded without resort to tender. We can look at two extremes to consider the possible implications for quality of construction work; what follows is somewhat simplistic but it is based on actual, if very limited, findings and serves to illustrate the point.

1. Firstly the conventional contractor based system. In any contract, time, cost and quality are interrelated; on minor urban infrastructure works, costs are controlled very tightly; overrun is 5%-10% only, whereas time overrun can be very large, commonly in excess of 50%. The contractor has to find the difference between costs as per Schedule of Rates and market rates; if the time overruns, this increases the cost of the work. In this situation, what 'gives' is the quality of the work, particularly skimping on materials. There is an extent to which this can be 'designed in' to the process through initial over-design and therefore inflating the estimated cost.
   Result: poor quality work cheap.

2. Secondly, the community-based system. There is no commonly accepted basis for estimating the costs where works are entrusted to community groups. In some situations it is argued that the terms offered to community groups are unduly favourable; in other situations community groups may incur cost overruns because of their lack of experience. Where the cost of the works is fixed, additional unpaid labour may be required to finish the works because of problems in execution. These costs may not be recovered and it may impact adversely on poor and vulnerable groups who make up the unskilled labour required for completion. However, the quality of the work is often good and is positively monitored by community groups in a way that contractors work is rarely supervised.
   Result: good quality work at a true cost which is difficult to determine, but in some cases may appear expensive.

3. The real problem occurs in those occasional situations where contractors appear in the guise of community groups in order to obtain more favourable financial terms for the construction. This is the worst of both worlds.
   Result: poor quality work which is expensive.

Quality control of the work may provide a means of addressing some of these issues.

- A means of monitoring construction quality involving users and beneficiaries is described in Box 5.1.
- Where Local Action Plans are being widely implemented on a city scale, there is scope for a powerful, independent monitoring committee with independent authority and technical expertise which has a remit to cover construction quality, financial transactions and deployment of labour.
- The opportunity to employ an independent engineer to act on behalf of users and beneficiaries; this provision now exists and is used by some groups in the Kerala Peoples Planning campaign in India.
- A standardised system for all items of work in a 'Standard Engineering Details' format whereby the cost of any item of work is simplified into a market rate estimate broken down into materials, skilled and unskilled labour; sketches are also provided.

The key point is that if the quality is monitored and controlled according to the Standard Engineering Detail specification, users actually get what they asked for and the money is being used for its intended purpose.
Result: value for money.

Community as advisers

Over twenty years the Calcutta Metropolitan Development Authority (CMDA) has evolved a system which involves the communities with councillors and contractors in a variety of ways in the slum improvement schemes funded by government and donors.

Box 5.1. Community as advisers

Narrative	Commentary
1. Project formulation involves consultation between the community, the CMDA and the Municipality about what facilities are to be provided within the budget. Clearly understood agreement is obtained before work starts.	■ The consultation involves the community, key local politicians and the engineering department.
2. The contractor is required to have a sample of his construction work (paving, pipe laying, concreting, etc.) approved by both the engineer and representatives of the community together. This sample of work becomes the yardstick against which the quality of the rest of the work can be judged. All parties, that is the community, the engineer and the contractor therefore have a point of reference against which future disagreements can be discussed and resolved.	■ CMDA places and enforces quite strict requirements on its contractors. Whilst this will be reflected in tender prices, they are getting added value in the form of improved overall management of the jobs. ■ The quality of work is excellent. ■ The community does not have a formal contractual role.
3. CMDA places great emphasis on completion testing, for example of pipelines. Certificated testing is incorporated into the contract and it is important that the contractor knows that it will be carried out in every case. Community representatives are invited to witness the testing so that they can see that it has been done.	

Monitoring: performance reporting systems

Performance reporting is an indispensable part of all management functions and provides the key input to performance evaluation. The relevant information can be classified as either an input to, or an output from, an activity or process as described in Box 5.2. Clarity and transparency are essential.

Box 5.2. Reporting

Input reporting

- Financial reporting of expenditure against budget (this may be allocated to separate heads for staff/labour costs and materials).
- Contract monitoring of the performance of external contractors.
- Consumption of materials and storekeeping records.

Output reporting

- The reporting of output is much less frequent; all to often, it is assumed that because the input has taken place, then the output must have been achieved. This is not so.
- Performance reporting of **output** i.e. verifying what has actually happened is therefore central.
- There are aspects of this which are necessarily subjective; in particular, it is important to realise that for provision of any service, we must obtain the perceptions of the users through participatory information gathering.

Note that community-based reporting has an important role to play, but will be much less formal; nevertheless, the principle of finding out and reporting on what is going on is an important factor in the eventual improvement of the services. (See Tools 1,3 and 5).

Performance reporting systems need to be developed in response to the particular needs of the programme and its financing agencies; it is not possible to generalise about specific systems. We can envisage information being consolidated at different levels:

- Specific neighbourhoods, in relation to inputs and outputs from the Local Action Plan; these can be consolidated at the Ward level into 'Ward at a glance' summary sheets which feed into the overall city summary.
- Area networked services; these are likely to be sector based and can also be consolidated at the Ward level into 'Ward at a glance' summary sheets which feed into the overall city summary.

An example is shown in Table 5.7. and Table 5.8.

Table 5.7. Example of monitoring summary for a local action plan

Local Action Plan	Ward/ Block/ Cluster	Work Order Ref	Sector	Infrastructure	Physical Estimated Quantities	Achieved	Contract Amount	Expenditure	% Physical Achievement	% Financial Achievement	Unit Costs as per Tender (Col 8/6)	Unit Costs as executed (Col 9/7)
1	2	3	4	5	6	7	8	9	10	11	12	13
1	18/I/1	2	Road	CC Road (Slab)	248	259	78445	82805	105%	106%	317	319
			Drain	Open Drains/ Brick	91	169	28638	39670	186%	139%	315	235
			Water	Stand Posts	5	8	22926	15094	160%	66%	4585	1887
				Water Supply lines								
			Sanitation	Toilets	8	8	144493	120406	100%	83%	18062	15051
				Bathrooms	5	2	44467	19820	40%	45%	8893	9910
				Urinals	5	2			40%			
Subtotal							**31869**	**277795**		**87%**		

Note: Currency in Rupees

Table 5.8. Example of abstracted monitoring information and 'Ward at a glance' summary

ABSTRACT OF WARD 18 Block I

Number of local action plans: 15

Sector	Inputs	Physical Target	Physical Achieved	Financial Target	Financial Achieved	%Physical target	%Financial target	Unit Cost-Estimated	Unit Cost-Executed
Roads	CC Road (Slab)	991.04	856.883	1021764	799846.5	86%	78%	1031.002	933.4372
	CC Pathway (IPS)	1752.37	1584.714	0	0	90%	0	0	0
Drain	Open Drains/ Brick	1254.5	1288.3	534750.1	567014	103%	106%	426.2655	440.1257
Water	Stand Posts	25	38	114267	74138.45	152%	65%	4570.68	1951.012
	Water Supply lines								
Sanitation	Toilets	55	45	993031.6	718554.9	82%	72%	18055.12	15967.89
	Bathrooms	20	14	210185.7	117467.8	70%	56%	10509.28	8390.554
	Urinals	24	5	0	0	21%		0	0
Total				2873998	2277022		79%		

Table 5.8. continued

Ward 18/I Abstract-At a Glance

Number of local action plans 15
Population of Ward 18/Block I 1277

	Estimated quantity	Actual quantity	Estimated Costs	Actual Costs
Roads	2.15	1.91	800.13	626.35
Drains	0.98	1.01	418.75	444.02
Water Stand Post	51.08 people per tap	33.6 per tap	89.48	58.06
Toilets	23.2 people per toilet	28.38 per toilet	777.63	562.69
Bathrooms	63.85 people per bath	91 per bath	164.59	91.99
			2250.59	1783.10

Note: quantities and costs are per capita values

Tool 15 Standard engineering details

What this tool will tell you

This tool will provide guidance on how to develop standard engineering details for use in an upgrading programme. It gives examples of the possible format and content.

How to use this tool

Standardised procedures have to be appropriate to the particular local circumstances. It is therefore not possible to prescribe exactly how both the engineering and the administrative aspects of these procedures and details need to be specified. Use the guidance points and the example to help you to decide what needs to be included in your standard details.

Note that having made the decision to use standard details, the sooner they are developed the better. This requires a concentrated input and it may be best to contract out some of the detailed work to local consultants.

Setting up a system for standard engineering details

A comprehensive library of standard engineering details (SEDs) which covers the likely infrastructure options is required. For each SED we need:

- engineering design & specification;
- professional quality draughting; and
- unit cost estimates.

The SEDs should follow a common format using the following information:

- allocate a unique reference code;
- define the unit of measurement;
- drawing of works (for example, see Figures P8 and P9);
- brief description of works;
- other SEDs commonly associated with this one;
- cost estimates (see Tool 16 for details); and
- reference to relevant items on Schedule of Rates (SoR).

See Table 15.2.

Table T15.1 gives a list of some of the items which could be included as SEDs.

Table T15.1. Examples of possible items suitable for standard engineering details	
Sector	**Standard Detail**
Ground preparation	General landfilling
Paving	Profiled gravel path CC paving with camber CC paving, reverse camber CC paving, reverse camber with centre drain Edging details
Drainage	Sullage type 1 (300 mm) Sullage type 2 (450 mm) Storm channel type 3 Compound section type 4 Stone pitching for natural channel sidewalls
Water Supply	Standpost with pipeline connection details, valvebox Handpump Apron type 1 Apron type 2 Pipe bedding Pipe jointing Small storage tank Bathing enclosure (example only; this is a case where users will specify design)
Sanitation	Sub structure for pour flush latrine Raised plinth/pit Septic tank 25-50 users Septic tank connection detail Superstructure ranges (katcha to pukka)
Solid waste	Small enclosure
Community buildings	Low cost open sided with end gables
Lighting	Pole mounted lantern Wall mounted lantern
Flood protection	RCC retaining wall Stone type 1 retaining wall Stone type 2 retaining wall

Table T15.2. Example of standard engineering details

Item	Concrete Lane Paving
Item Code	Programme Ref/SED/P1
Unit of measurement	1 square metre surface area
Description	100 mm thickness of Cement Concrete 1:2:4 using graded broken stone of size 40 mm and 20 mm in the ratio 50:50 including boxing, watering, curing etc. complete.
Reference to SoR	See Item 622
Associated Items	Formation and filling Programme Ref/SED/F1

Table T15.3. Example of other associated standard engineering details

Drawings	Description/Application
UP/SED/P1/1	Paved lane: conventional camber
UP/SED/P1/2	Paved lane: road-as-drain, reverse camber
UP/SED/P1/3	
etc.	

Tool 16 Spreadsheets for cost estimation

What this tool will tell you

This tool provides specific guidance on the development and presentation of cost estimates in order to simplify the procedures for moving from Local Action Plans to implementation of construction. It gives detailed guidance on:

- developing cost information which users can understand; and
- developing cost information for use in obtaining approvals and sanctions.

How to use this tool

This tool is based on the use of personal computer spreadsheets; these are an ideal tool for cost estimation because they permit unit costs to be changed easily and the subsequent calculations for total costs are then done automatically. This tool uses examples to illustrate how spreadsheets can be used to help you with cost estimation using both the Schedule of Rates and Market Rates. These spreadsheets are then further developed to lead to the most important results of this tool, namely to develop appropriate cost information for both service users and for obtaining the necessary procedural approvals.

Refer back to Tables 5.3, 5.4. and 5.5 for background information.

Making use of spreadsheets

Table 5.4 describes how different groups of stakeholders need information about costs which are expressed in different ways. In summary:

- Engineers in government departments need to know the cost based on the current Schedule of Rates;
- local user groups, communities and donors need to know the cost based on the current market rate; and
- local user groups need the market rate cost information to be expressed in a way which is very easy to understand; the format of the estimates produced by engineers are unintelligible to the public at large and this is not acceptable in the context of local action planning.

Schedule of Rates

Table T16.1 presents an example of a cost estimate for concrete lane paving; printed from a Microsoft Excel spreadsheet. This has been split into materials and labour. If this is set up on a spreadsheet with the appropriate instructions, whenever the values in the "SoR" (Schedule of Rates) column are altered the values in the "Amount" column are automatically recalculated with the new SoR values.

Table T16.1. Cost estimation spreadsheet according to SoR

Materials cost PROGRAMME REF/SED/P1

Quantity	Unit	Material	SoR 1996 Rs-Ps	Per	Amount Rs-Ps
0.0475	cubic metre	40 mm metal	162.50	cubic metre	7.72
0.045	cubic metre	20 mm metal	234.00	cubic metre	10.53
0.0925	cubic metre	conveyance (metal)	126.75	cubic metre	11.72
0.0465	cubic metre	sand	78.00	cubic metre	3.63
0.0465	cubic metre	conveyance (sand)	85.72	cubic metre	3.99
33	Kg	cement	2600.00	Tonne	85.80
33	kg	conveyance (cement)	60.49	Tonne	2.00

Total materials cost per square metre of surfacing	**125.38**

Labour cost PROGRAMME REF/SED/P1

Quantity	Unit	Description	SoR 1996 Rs-Ps	Per	Amount Rs-Ps
0.015	Days	Mason	84.00	Day	1.26
0.100	Days	Man Labour	56.70	Day	5.67
0.245	Days	Woman Labour	46.20	Day	11.32

Total labour cost per square metre of surfacing	**18.25**

Total cost (SoR 1996) PROGRAMME REF/SED/P1

Total materials plus labour cost per square metre of surfacing	143.63
Add 10% contingencies	14.36
Total cost per square metre of surfacing	**157.99**

Market rates

Another copy of the spreadsheet in Table T16.1 can be used to input similar details but using the market rates rather than the Schedule of Rates as shown in Table T16.2. The "rates" column will require regular updating, possibly on a monthly basis if construction prices are rising rapidly.

Table T16.2. Market rate estimation and cost index

Materials cost   PROGRAMME REF/SED/P1

		Date	XXXX	Valid until	YYYY
Quantity	Unit	Material	Rate RS-Ps	Per	Amount Rs-Ps
0.0475	cubic metre	40 mm metal	166.00	cubic metre	7.89
0.045	cubic metre	20 mm metal	250.00	cubic metre	11.25
0.0925	cubic metre	conveyance (metal)	126.75	cubic metre	11.72
0.0465	cubic metre	sand	78.00	cubic metre	3.63
0.0465	cubic metre	conveyance (sand)	85.72	cubic metre	3.99
33	kg	cement	2800.00	Tonne	92.40
33	kg	conveyance (cement)	60.49	Tonne	2.00
Total materials cost per square metre of surfacing					**132.87**

Labour cost   PROGRAMME REF/SED/P1

Quantity	Unit	Description	Rate RS-Ps	Per	Amount Rs-Ps
0.015	Days	Mason	100.00	Days	1.50
0.100	Days	Man Labour	56.70	Days	5.67
0.245	Days	Woman Labour	46.20	Days	11.32
Total labour cost per square metre of surfacing					**18.49**

Total cost   PROGRAMME REF/SED/P1

Total materials plus labour cost per square metre of surfacing	151.36
Add 10% contingencies	15.14
Total cost per square metre of surfacing	**166.49**

Cost information for user groups and communities

Cost estimates based on the market rates as shown by the example of Table T16.2 are for unit costs; these need to be further processed to build up a clearer picture of the actual total costs for carrying out work specified in the Local Action Plan. This involves multiplying unit rates by the quantity of work to be done and the spreadsheet can easily be adapted for this. Remember that the most important point about spreadsheets is that they enable changes to be calculated very simply. The spreadsheet shown in Table T16.3 gives an example.

Table T16.3. Combining unit cost estimates with information from Local Action Plans

Slum AA Nagar: concrete paving details abstracted from Local Action Plan

Concrete lane paving			Labour		
Lane	Length	Paved Width	Male labour	Female labour	Skilled
No	metres	metres	Days	Days	Days
2	10	1.5	1.5	3.7	0.2
3	20	1.5	3	7.4	0.5
4	15	1.5	2.3	5.5	0.3
5	150	3	45	110.2	6.8
6			0	0	0
7			0	0	0
Totals			52	127	8

Table T16.3. (continued)

Concrete lane paving — Materials

Lane No	Length	Paved Width	Sand		40mm metal		20mm metal		Cement	
	metres	metres	Quantity cubic m	Cost Rs	Quantity cubic m	Cost Rs	Quantity cubic m	Cost Rs	Quantity Tonne	Cost Rs
2	10	1.5	0.70	114	0.71	206	0.675	243	0.495	1316
3	20	1.5	1.395	228	1.425	412	1.35	487	0.99	2633
4	15	1.5	1.046	171	1.068	309	1.012	365	0.742	1975
5	150	3	20.9	3425	21.3	6182	20.25	7305	14.85	39508
6										
7										
Totals Quantity			24.06		24.58		23.29		17.08	
Totals Cost				3948		7109		8400		45432

Total materials cost for AA Nagar paving   Rs 64 889

It is also easy to express the quantities of materials in a way which people may understand more easily. For example, cement often comes in 50kg bags; sand and road metal may be delivered by small trucks which carry say 3 cubic metres. The materials component of Table T16.3 can be developed in this way if necessary.

Table T16.3. (continued)						
Lane No	Length metres	Paved Width metres	Sand Quantity Truck loads	40mm metal Quantity Truck loads	20mm metal Quantity Truck loads	Cement Quantity Bags
2	10	1.5	0.23	0.24	0.23	10
3	20	1.5	0.47	0.48	0.45	20
4	15	1.5	0.35	0.36	0.34	15
5	150	3	7	7.1	6.75	297
Totals	Quantity		8	8.18	7.76	342

This is just an example. The key point is

- find out what units of measurement user groups and residents are most familiar with and use those to explain the quantities and costs involved.

Cost information for approvals and sanctions

The information in the basic spreadsheets for unit cost estimates according to the Schedule of Rates and Market Rates can easily be developed to make the formal procedures relatively straightforward. There are several stages which can all help to make things easier.

Stage 1: prepare a spreadsheet summarising the unit cost estimates for all SEDs using both the Schedule of Rates and the Market Rates which have already been approved by the required competent authority. This summary requires updating regularly as described earlier; an example is shown in Table T16.4 below.

Table T16.4. Preparation of summary unit costs for SEDs				
Dates applicable from: dd/mm/yy to: dd/mm/yy				
Sector	**Item**	**Unit**	**Market Rate Rs-Ps**	**Schedule of Rates Rs-Ps**
Ground Prep.	PROGRAMME REF/SED/G1	cubic metre	XX-yy	AA-bb
Paving	PROGRAMME REF/SED/P1	square metre	XX-yy	AA-bb
	PROGRAMME REF/SED/P2	square metre	XX-yy	AA-bb
Drainage	PROGRAMME REF/SED/D1	metre	XX-yy	AA-bb
	PROGRAMME REF/SED/D2	metre	XX-yy	AA-bb
	PROGRAMME REF/SED/D3	metre	XX-yy	AA-bb
	PROGRAMME REF/SED/D4	metre	XX-yy	AA-bb
Water	PROGRAMME REF/SED/W1	number	XX-yy	AA-bb
	PROGRAMME REF/SED/W2	number	XX-yy	AA-bb
	PROGRAMME REF/SED/W3	metre	XX-yy	AA-bb
	PROGRAMME REF/SED/W4	number	XX-yy	AA-bb
Lighting	PROGRAMME REF/SED/L1	number	XX-yy	AA-bb
Solid waste	PROGRAMME REF/SED/M1	number	XX-yy	AA-bb
MCF	PROGRAMME REF/SED/C1	number	XX-yy	AA-bb
	PROGRAMME REF/SED/C2	number	XX-yy	AA-bb

Stage 2: use this summarised information to develop a further spreadsheet which details the costs for all of the items in a particular Local Action Plan. Ideally this should be used to obtain the necessary financial sanctions for implementation of the work. An example is shown in Table T16.5. Note that it is not possible to prescribe exactly the format in which the information needs to be presented; that is determined by local practice. This example serves to illustrate the approach; you can 'customise' spreadsheets to suit the local administrative needs. Some Local Action Plans will specify improvements for which there are no SEDs; in this case, separate approval will need to be granted if finance is channelled via a government department. We have also

included a financial statement on the spreadsheet below which specifies who is contributing what to the overall cost. For programmes which involve finance via a government department, it needs to be made clear that the proposed expenditure is within the particular budget limit for the neighbourhood or user group.

Note: Illustrative only: do not use

Table T16.5. Example: Cost estimate prepared for procedural approval

Slum Name	AA Nagar	No families	100
Slum Code	0001	Population	600

Section 1   Standard Items

Sector	Item	Unit	Quantity	Schedule of Rates Rs-Ps	Cost Estimate using Schedule of Rates Rs-Ps	Market rates Rs-Ps	Cost Estimate using Market Rates Rs-Ps
Ground Prep	PROGRAMME REF/SED/G1	cubic metre	35	1000	35000	1100	38500
Paving	PROGRAMME REF/SED/P1	square metre	200	1000	200000	1100	220000
	PROGRAMME REF/SED/P2	square metre	150	1000	150000	1100	165000
Drainage	PROGRAMME REF/SED/D1	metre	80	1000	80000	1100	88000
	PROGRAMME REF/SED/D2	metre	35	1000	35000	1100	38500
	PROGRAMME REF/SED/D3	metre	30	1000	30000	1100	33000
	PROGRAMME REF/SED/D4	metre	20	1000	20000	1100	22000
Water	PROGRAMME REF/SED/W2	number	2	1000	2000	1100	2200
	PROGRAMME REF/SED/W3	number	3	1000	3000	1100	3300
Lighting	PROGRAMME REF/SED/L1	number	14	1000	14000	1100	15400
Solid waste	PROGRAMME REF/SED/M1	number	3	1000	3000	1100	3300
Community Building	PROGRAMME REF/SED/C1	plinth area, square metres	50	1000	50000	1100	55000
Sub Totals					622000		684200

Section 2   **Cost approval check**

Budget ceiling amount based on Rs 1200 per capita	720000
Gross Estimate Amount, Schedule of Rates	622000
Gross Estimate Amount, Market Rates	684200
User contributions: community building	10000
Net Estimate Amount, Schedule of Rates	612000
Net estimate Amount, Market Rates	674200

Note on approval basis

1. Both Net Estimate amounts to be less than/equal to budget ceiling amount

Printed in the USA
CPSIA information can be obtained
at www.ICGtesting.com
JSHW052020140824
68134JS00027B/2568

9 780906 055823